Saved Personal Bible Study

Saved Personal Bible Study

Experiencing the Promise of the Book of Acts

Nancy Guthrie

:: CROSSWAY®

WHEATON, ILLINOIS

Saved Personal Bible Study: Experiencing the Promise of the Book of Acts

© 2024 by Nancy Guthrie

Published by Crossway
        1300 Crescent Street
        Wheaton, Illinois 60187

Cover design: Crystal Courtney

First printing 2024

Printed in China

Trade paperback ISBN: 978-1-4335-9494-6
ePub ISBN: 978-1-4335-9496-0
PDF ISBN: 978-1-4335-9495-3

Crossway is a publishing ministry of Good News Publishers.

RRD			33	32	31	30	29	28	27	26	25	24
15	14	13	12	11	10	9	8	7	6	5	4	3	2

Contents

A Note from Nancy

I'm so glad you're planning to work your way through this study of the book of Acts! The following personal Bible study questions are intended to help you get the most out of each chapter in the book or video session. I suggest that you work through them *before* you read each chapter or watch each video. You'll get far more out of what I present if you do.

You may choose to do each personal Bible study lesson in one sitting, or you might want to plan on doing a couple of questions each day during the week so that you have some time in the Bible every day. As you study, understand that the goal is not to get the "right answer." If some of the questions seem difficult (and some of them may be!), please know that my aim is not to frustrate you or to make you flip back and forth in your Bible as busywork. My aim is to get you into the text of Acts, thinking deeply about what is transpiring in this story and how it fits into God's salvation plans for history and for his people.

You may be left wondering at times why I've asked certain questions, or feel like some things are still unclear. If you find there are questions you can't completely answer, that's okay! This personal Bible study is just one part of the learning process. Some of the questions serve to lay the groundwork for what I will explain more fully in the chapters or video sessions. Hopefully my purpose in certain questions will become clear when you read each chapter or watch the videos, and even more clear as you discuss them with your group. Working through the text in advance using these questions will equip you to grasp more fully what is being taught in the corresponding book chapter or video session.

You'll find that this personal Bible study is primarily focused on helping you dig into and understand the text itself—what it says and what it means. Often we want to put in a few minutes of Bible reading and come away with a feel-good bit of encouragement or a clear to-do list. We want a quick "How does this apply to my life?" takeaway. Applying the Bible to our lives is indeed essential! But appropriate applications or implications are not always immediately clear. We're going to find throughout Acts that much of the narrative is more descriptive than prescriptive, with broad takeaways from the book as a whole. It's good for us to press in and think deeply to gain clarity about what the text meant to the original audience, and how it relates to the larger story of redemption through Christ, before we bring it into our own context.

You'll find that I've included maps along the way for you to identify countries and cities in the story of Acts and to trace where various characters take the gospel. My hope is that these exercises will help you visualize the action and gain a firmer grip on the progression of the story being told in Acts.

A first question for many people is, How long should these questions take to answer? There is no set time frame. Each lesson has nine to twelve questions. Some of them require more reading in other parts of the Bible than others. I would hope that you would be able to read the pertinent passages and complete the questions in thirty to sixty minutes each week.

We're all different in the way we approach a page of questions and blank space for answers. Some of us are brief, jotting down a few words that may represent more comprehensive thoughts and ideas that we might share verbally with a group. Others of us want to record a thorough written answer to every question. I hope you'll feel the freedom to do what works for you. I've sought to include enough space on these pages to record the answer I came up with for each question as I created it. And my answers are usually brief.

Certainly some weeks you will have more time than others, but we all know that we get more out of study if we put more into it. What is most important is not how much time you take but taking the time to work through the personal Bible study and keeping that appointment. You may want to write down at the bottom of this page when you plan to work on these questions each week, making an appointment with yourself. And I hope you'll keep it! I think one of the best times to work on something like this is on Sunday afternoon or evening. It's the Lord's Day. Spending time engaging with him through his word is a wonderful way to make the most of his day and to make sure you get your lesson done each week.

Another particular challenge with this study will simply be to keep going. Acts is the longest book in the New Testament. We will cover its twenty-eight chapters over seventeen lessons (the introduction session has no personal Bible study). I hope you will decide now to persevere to the end so that after you've completed the study, you'll have a firm grip on the events of the initial spread of the gospel from Jerusalem, to Judea and Samaria, and to the end of the earth. More than that, I hope that persevering through the study will fill you with a sense of confidence that God's purposes of salvation in this world are unstoppable.

If you are reading the book or watching the videos with a group, I suggest you bring your copy of these answered questions when your group meets. As your leader works through the discussion questions that are provided in the leader's guide, he or she may bring in some (but not all) of these personal Bible study questions. Having them with you will also give you the opportunity to ask other group members for help with any questions you struggled to answer.

I'm convinced that God works through his word. The Holy Spirit uses the written word to open our eyes, to change our perspectives, and nurture our love for Christ. I pray that he will use your time in his word to do exactly that. And I pray that as you seek to grasp the significance of what Luke recorded for us in the pages of Acts, you'll grow in your confidence that God still works by his Spirit through his word to add to his church. I pray you'll believe more deeply than ever that his gospel is what the world most needs to hear. And I hope you'll be filled with gratitude for what God has done to make his gospel known to the ends of the earth—and more specifically, to you.

Warmly,

Nancy Guthrie

Lesson 1

You Will Be My Witnesses

ACTS 1:1–26

1. Read Acts 1:1–3, which serves as a summary of what Luke wrote in the Gospel of Luke and what he is going to write in this first chapter of Acts. When you read that Jesus spent forty days "speaking about the kingdom of God" with the apostles, what kinds of things do you think he might have discussed? (You might also want to read Luke 24:44–48, which provides another statement about what Jesus taught the apostles, or use your concordance to find other passages that refer to the kingdom.)

2. Read Acts 1:4. Jesus tells the disciples to wait for "the promise of the Father." What do the following verses reveal about this promise?

   Isaiah 32:14–15:

   Isaiah 44:3:

   Joel 2:28–29:

3. Read Acts 1:6–7. The disciples' question, "Lord, will you at this time restore the kingdom to Israel?" could be understood a number of ways. How would the following passages have shaped the disciples' expectations of "restoration"?

   Isaiah 49:5–6:

   Ezekiel 37:20–28:

Zechariah 2:10–11:

_____

_____

4. Read Acts 1:8, which provides a rough outline for the entire book of Acts. Consider who Jesus was speaking to. Why might this statement from Jesus have been challenging for them to grasp?

_____

_____

_____

_____

5. Read Acts 1:9–11. What details do these verses provide about the ascension and return of Christ?

_____

_____

_____

_____

6. Read Acts 3:19–21. What does Peter come to understand about the time of restoration?

_____

_____

7. Read Acts 1:12–20. In verse 16, Peter says that the psalms of David he is quoting (Psalms 69:25 and 109:8) are fulfilled in

Judas. How do you think Peter has been able to come to that conclusion? (See Luke 24:25–27, 44–47.)

8. Read Acts 1:21–26. What requirements do you find for the replacement apostle according to these verses? (You might also consult Acts 10:39–41.)

9. The time the apostles spent with Jesus between his resurrection and ascension helped them to grapple with the ways the kingdom of Jesus was not what they had expected it to be. They had to make some adjustments in their understanding and expectations. Has your life, as a citizen of the kingdom of God, been what you expected it to be? What truths from Jesus's teaching about the kingdom could help you adjust your expectations toward what Jesus has promised?

I Will Pour Out My Spirit

ACTS 2:1–47

1. Read Acts 2:1. The events of this chapter take place on "the day of Pentecost" (2:1), one of numerous Old Testament feasts. To see the significance of this, it's helpful to review some other feasts and how they were brought to ultimate fulfillment in Jesus Christ. The original Passover recalled the sacrifice of the lambs in Egypt (Ex. 12), but it pointed forward to Jesus, who was sacrificed as the Lamb of God on Passover (Luke 22:7). On the first day after the Sabbath of Passover week was the Feast of Firstfruits (Lev. 23:9–11), in which Israelites offered the first of their harvest to God. And three days after his death, Jesus rose from the grave as the "firstfruits of those who have fallen asleep" (1 Cor. 15:20–23).

   Then seven weeks after the Feast of Firstfruits came the Feast of Weeks, also called the Feast of Harvest (Ex. 23:16) or

Pentecost, which celebrated the completion or fullness of the harvest. And what we read about in Acts 2 takes place seven weeks after Jesus's resurrection, on Pentecost. Skip ahead to Acts 2:41. What kind of harvest is celebrated on this day of Pentecost?

2. Read Acts 2:2–4. The 120 believers gathered in the room hear a sound "like a mighty rushing wind" and see "divided tongues as of fire." Numerous times throughout Old Testament history there was wind or fire as heavenly and earthly realms came together. What examples do you find in the following verses?

Exodus 3:2:

Exodus 14:21:

Exodus 19:18:

Job 38:1:

_____

_____

Ezekiel 1:4:

_____

_____

3. What do you think is the significance of the fire appearing as tongues in this instance?

_____

_____

_____

4. Read Acts 2:5–13. On this map, circle all of the countries or areas from which Jews have gathered in Jerusalem for the feast of Pentecost.

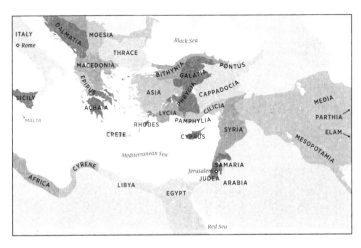

5. Read Acts 2:14–21. What do you think Peter is trying to communicate by connecting what is happening at Pentecost to Joel's prophecy? How would this be different from what a few Old Testament believers experienced to accomplish particular tasks (for example, Bezalel in Ex. 31:1–5; Balaam in Num. 24:2; Saul in 1 Sam. 10:10; and Daniel in Dan. 4:8)?

6. The prophecy in Joel is typical of lots of Old Testament prophecy in that it foresees future events that are separated by time, but speaks of them as one event. Part of Joel's prophecy is being fulfilled at Pentecost, but what still-future event is described in Acts 2:19–21?

7. Read Acts 2:22–32. What event does Peter say David wrote about in the Psalms that could not have been about David?

8. Read Acts 2:33–36. What events does Peter say David wrote about in Psalm 110?

9. Read Acts 2:37–41. Peter says that those who repent and are baptized will receive the gift of the Holy Spirit. How do you see the power of the Spirit at work in the following verses?

v. 36:

v. 37:

v. 38:

v. 39:

v. 41:

_____

_____

10. Read Acts 2:42–47. The Spirit's power might seem most obvious in the "wonders and signs" the apostles were doing. But how else do you see the power of the Spirit at work in these verses?

v. 42:

_____

_____

v. 43:

_____

_____

v. 45:

_____

_____

vv. 45–46:

_____

_____

v. 47:

_____

_____

11. In this passage, we see the impact of the Holy Spirit's coming on and in the first believers. In what ways has the Holy Spirit moved powerfully in your life? What are some ways you would like to see the Holy Spirit work further in your life?

Lesson 3

In Jesus the Resurrection from the Dead

ACTS 3:1–4:31

1. Read through the following passages from the Old Testament
   prophets. What do they have in common?

Then the eyes of the blind shall be opened,
   and the ears of the deaf unstopped;
then shall the lame man leap like a deer,
   and the tongue of the mute sing for joy.
For waters break forth in the wilderness,
   and streams in the desert (Isa. 35:5–6)

Behold, I will bring them from the north country
   and gather them from the farthest parts of the earth,
among them the blind and the lame,

the pregnant woman and she who is in labor, together;
    a great company, they shall return here. (Jer. 31:8)

"Behold, at that time I will deal
    with all your oppressors.
And I will save the lame
    and gather the outcast,
and I will change their shame into praise
    and renown in all the earth.
At that time I will bring you in,
    at the time when I gather you together;
for I will make you renowned and praised
    among all the peoples of the earth,
when I restore your fortunes
    before your eyes," says the Lord. (Zeph. 3:19–20)

In that day, declares the Lord,
    I will assemble the lame
and gather those who have been driven away
    and those whom I have afflicted;
and the lame I will make the remnant,
    and those who were cast off, a strong nation;
and the Lord will reign over them in Mount Zion
    from this time forth and forevermore. (Mic. 4:6–7)

2. Read Acts 3:1–10. How does this story connect to the prophetic passages you've just read?

3. Read Acts 3:11–26. How would you summarize Peter's argument in this sermon?

4 . Read Acts 3:11–26, in which Peter speaks about who Jesus is and what he does. What things in these verses do you think would have been especially difficult for Peter's audience to hear? What would they have found encouraging to hear?

Difficult to hear:

_____

_____

Encouraging to hear:

_____

_____

_____

_____

5. Read Acts 4:1–4. How does Luke summarize what Peter and John were teaching (v. 2)? How do those who heard it respond?

_____

_____

_____

_____

6. Read the following Old Testament passages and note a phrase from each that would have shaped what Peter's listeners would have understood or expected regarding "the resurrection from the dead."

Job 19:25–27:

_____

_____

Isaiah 25:6–9:

Isaiah 26:19:

Daniel 12:2:

7. Read Acts 4:5–12. Peter and John are interrogated by the rulers, elders, scribes, and the entire high priestly family, including Annas (the high priest) and Caiaphas. For what "crime" are they examining Peter and John? What accusations does Peter make against them?

8. Read Acts 4:13–22. How does this passage connect to Acts 1:8: "But you will receive power when the Holy Spirit has come

17

upon you, and you will be my witnesses in Jerusalem and in all Judea and Samaria, and to the end of the earth"?

9. Read Acts 4:23–31. How do the believers relate Psalm 2 to what Peter and John have just experienced? How does the quote from Psalm 2 relate to the statement in 4:28?

10. Peter and John are incredibly bold in speaking of Christ despite the pressures of the religious leaders. In verse 29, we read that they prayed for boldness to keep speaking the word of God. How would you rate your own boldness in speaking of Christ? What do you think it would look like for you to be bold? Are you willing to pray for boldness?

You Will Not Be Able to Overthrow Them

ACTS 4:32–5:42

1. Read Acts 4:32–36. How would you characterize what is "great" or impressive in the following verses?

   v. 33a:

   _____

   _____

   v. 33b:

   _____

   _____

   vv. 32, 34–35:

   _____

   _____

YOU WILL NOT BE ABLE TO OVERTHROW THEM

2. Read Acts 5:1–11. How are Ananias and Sapphira's actions characterized in verse 3?

How are their actions characterized in verse 9?

Why do you think Ananias and Sapphira do this?

3. Like Ananias and Sapphira, we too face the temptation of seeking to appear more spiritual or sacrificial than we actually are. Can you identify any specific ways or situations in which you face this temptation? What changes might you need to make in order to be more truthful with how you present your devotion to and relationship with Christ?

4. Read Acts 5:12–17. Why do you think the high priest and the rest of the religious council respond this way to the signs and wonders of the apostles?

And where have we heard this before? (See Matt. 27:18.)

5. Read Acts 5:18–32. How is the charge to the apostles from the angel who brought them out of prison the exact opposite of the charge to the apostles from the religious council?

6. After the council charges them not to teach about the gospel, they immediately announce the gospel to the council. What are the key elements of the gospel, according to verses 30–32?

7. Read Acts 5:33–39. In verse 39, Gamaliel makes a profound statement. We are still early in the book of Acts, but from what you know about how the story will progress, how will his statement prove true in this book?

8. Read Acts 5:40–42. Notice what they are instructed to do and what they actually do. What do you think generates the joy and persistence in these apostles?

9. Being beaten for speaking of Christ is likely outside of your experience, but suffering dishonor for speaking about or identifying with Jesus may not be. How difficult is it for you to imagine rejoicing in that? What fueled the apostles' rejoicing that could also enable you to rejoice?

Lesson 5

The Most High Does Not Dwell in Houses Made by Hands

ACTS 6:1–7:60

1. Read Acts 6:1–7. According to verse 1 and verse 7, what is increasing?

_____

_____

What is the threat to the increase in these verses?

_____

_____

2. Read Acts 6:7–12. What do you find in the following verses that might have generated anger toward Stephen and the gospel he was preaching among the Jews in Jerusalem?

v. 7:

v. 8:

v. 10:

3. Read Acts 6:13–15. How would you summarize the charges against Stephen? How is what happens in verse 15 ironic in light of those charges? (See Ex. 34:29–35.)

4. Read Acts 7:1–8. According to verse 2, where was the glory of God with Abraham?

5. Read Acts 7:9–16. According to verse 9, where was the presence of God with Joseph?

_____

6. Read Acts 7:17–36. According to verse 30, where was the glory of God with Moses?

_____

7. Read Acts 7:37–43. Why do you think Stephen mentions in verse 39 that Moses was rejected by the people?

_____

_____

_____

_____

Why might Stephen specifically mention Aaron, the first high priest, leading the people into idolatry (v. 40)?

_____

_____

_____

_____

8. Read Acts 7:44–47. Where was the glory of God in Moses's day, in Joshua's day, in David's day, and in Solomon's day?

Moses's day (v. 44):

_____

_____

Joshua's day (v. 45):

David's day (v. 45):

Solomon's day (v. 47):

9. Read Acts 7:48–50. According to Stephen, who quotes from Psalm 11 and Isaiah 66, where does God not dwell?

10. Read Acts 7:51–53. How would you summarize Stephen's final indictment of the religious leaders?

11. Read Acts 7:54–60. How is Stephen's declaration of what he sees a fitting conclusion to the argument he's been making?

12. Following Stephen's interaction with his accusers and tracing his argument in this passage is rather challenging. Hopefully it will become clearer as you read Nancy's chapter or watch the video session. It ends, however, with the sad and yet victorious event of the stoning of Stephen. What aspects of the way Stephen faces death would you hope to emulate when facing death?

Lesson 6

They Were All Scattered

ACTS 8:1–40

1. Read Acts 7:59–8:4. How is the persecution that comes upon
   the church after the death of Stephen a demonstration or il-
   lustration of Joseph's words to his brothers in Genesis 50:20:
   "As for you, you meant evil against me, but God meant it for
   good, to bring it about that many people should be kept alive,
   as they are today"?

   _____

   _____

   _____

   _____

2. Read Luke 9:51–56 and John 4:5–9. How does seeing the
   attitude of the apostles toward Samaritans in these passages

help us to understand the significance of what we read in Acts 8:5–8?

3. Read Acts 8:9–13. What are some key differences between Simon and Philip? Pay special attention to the words or concepts that show up in both the description of Simon (vv. 9–11) and the description of Philip (vv. 12–13).

4. Read Acts 8:14–17. Why would it have been important for the apostles to witness the Samaritans receiving the Holy Spirit in a way similar to the experience of believers in Jerusalem on Pentecost?

5. Read Acts 8:18–24. Commentators disagree regarding whether or not Simon came to genuine faith in Christ. What evidence do you see for and against it here?

6. Read Acts 8:25. What aspect of Jesus's command in Acts 1:8 are they fulfilling?

7. Read Acts 8:26–28. What do you think this Gentile eunuch likely experienced when he went to the temple in Jerusalem? (See Deut. 23:1 for help.)

8. How might the Ethiopian eunuch have found hope in the following Old Testament passages? (Note that Cush is the ancient name for the territory of the Ethiopians.)

Psalm 68:31:

Psalm 87:4:

Isaiah 56:3–5:

9. Read Acts 8:29–38 along with Isaiah 53. Philip tells the eunuch the good news about Jesus based on the passage he is reading in Isaiah 53. What might Philip have said about Jesus based on Isaiah 53?

10. In this chapter, Philip takes the gospel to people he would have avoided all his life. Are there any types or categories of people you would find it especially hard to share Christ with? What do you think it would take for you to move toward such people in love?

Lesson 7

God's Chosen Instrument

ACTS 9:1–31

1. What do we learn about Saul's background from the following passages?

Philippians 3:4–6:

_____

_____

Acts 7:57–8:3:

_____

_____

Acts 22:3–5:

_____

_____

2. How do Leviticus 24:16 and John 16:2–3 help us to understand what motivates Saul in his rage against those who put their faith in Jesus?

3. Read Acts 9:1–2. What words would you use to describe Saul's attitude and actions?

4. Read Acts 9:3–9. Why would it be devastating for Saul to hear that the person speaking to him out of the radiant, blinding light from heaven is Jesus of Nazareth?

5. According to 1 Corinthians 9:1 and Acts 9:27, what or who creates the blinding light that temporarily blinds Saul?

6. Read Acts 9:10–22. While something supernatural is happening to Saul on the road to Damascus, something supernatural is also happening to Ananias in Damascus. What happens, and why do you think it is necessary?

7. What do you think Ananias and the other disciples of Jesus in Damascus must have thought and felt when they heard Saul declaring in the synagogue that Jesus was the Son of God?

8. What is emphasized in both Acts 9:15 and Galatians 1:11–16 about Paul's ministry?

9. Read Acts 9:23–31. What is ironic in this passage in terms of what is happening to the man who sought to kill followers of Jesus?

10. To the Christians in his day, Saul must have seemed like the last person in the world who would ever become a Christian. Are there any people like that in your world? Spend some time praying that the same Jesus who revealed himself to Saul would reveal himself to those who are blind to who he is.

Lesson 8

What God Has Made Clean

ACTS 9:32–11:18

1. Read Acts 9:32–35 and Luke 5:18–26. What similarities do you see between the healing Jesus performed in Luke's Gospel and the healing Jesus performed through Peter?

_____

_____

_____

_____

2. Read Acts 9:36–42 and Mark 5:35–43. What similarities do you see between the healing Jesus performed in Mark's Gospel and the healing Jesus performed through Peter?

_____

_____

What is the big difference at the end?

3. Why do you think Luke might have told the stories about the miracles Peter performed in such a similar way to the stories of Jesus's earlier miracles?

4. Read Acts 10:1–8. Cornelius is a Gentile, but he is not like most Gentiles. What sets him apart from most Gentiles and makes him similar to the Ethiopian eunuch we met in chapter 8?

5. To understand why Peter's vision and experience in Acts 10 is so significant, we have to go back to the Mosaic law. Skim Leviticus 11:1–19, 45–47. Then read Exodus 19:4–6; Deuteronomy 4:5–8; and Jeremiah 33:8–9. What do these passages reveal about God's purpose in setting apart the Israelites to be his "treasured possession" from among the nations and giving them the holiness laws in Leviticus?

6. What practical effect would the food laws have had on Jewish interaction with Gentiles?

7. Read Acts 10:9–16. In light of what you read in Leviticus 11, why do you think the divine voice repeats his instruction to Peter three times?

8. Read Acts 10:17–23. What do you think would have happened differently if Peter had not just received the vision from God?

9. Read Acts 10:24–33. What does Peter's statement in verse 28 reveal about how he has interpreted the vision given to him in Joppa?

10. Read Peter's gospel announcement to the Gentiles gathered in Cornelius's home in Acts 10:34–43. What are the key elements of his gospel presentation?

11. Read Acts 10:44–48. If the Gentiles who believe the gospel receive the same gift as the Jews who believed the gospel back in Acts 2, what does this mean for the future of the new-covenant community?

12. Read Acts 11:1–18. How does the attitude of some of the Jews in Jerusalem change from verse 2 to verse 18?

13. Acts 11:18 celebrates that God has granted the Gentiles "repentance that leads to life." How would you define *repentance*? In what ways does it lead to life? How have you personally experienced repentance leading to life?

Lesson 9

The Hand of the Lord
Was with Them

ACTS 11:19–12:25

1. Read Acts 11:19–20. Note these locations on a map. Up to
   this point, the Jewish believers have been preaching Christ to
   Jews and God-fearing Gentiles (such as the Ethiopian eunuch
   and Cornelius). But as the gospel spreads out from Jerusalem
   geographically, it is also spreading out in terms of the people
   who are hearing it. What kind of people are now hearing the
   gospel, according to these verses?

2. Read Acts 11:19–26. Use the following chart to compare what happens as pagan Gentiles believe in Christ to what happened in Acts 8, when Samaritans believed in Christ.

	Acts 8 (Samaria)	Acts 11 (Antioch)
What precipitates the believers' departure from Jerusalem	A great persecution arises against the church after the stoning of Stephen. (8:1)	
The kind of people to whom they present Christ	Philip preaches Christ to Samaritans (people who were partly Jewish). (8:4–6)	
The response to their message	Crowds listen and believe and are baptized. (8:12)	
Apostolic authentication and support from Jerusalem elders	Peter and John are sent from Jerusalem to verify that Samaritans have become believers in Christ, to pray for them, and to lay hands on them to receive the Holy Spirit. (8:14–17)	

3. Read Acts 11:27–30. What evidence do you see in these verses that the Spirit is at work in Antioch?

_____

_____

4. Read Acts 12:1–5. How is Herod Agrippa's treatment of James and Peter similar to the way Jesus was treated by Herod Antipas and Pilate in terms of motive, timing, and guarding?

Pilate agreed to kill Jesus to please the Jews. Herod Antipas wanted to kill Jesus. (Mark 15:15; Luke 13:31)

The arrest and killing of Jesus took place during the days of Unleavened Bread and Passover, motivated in part by Pilate's desire to appear to honor these Jewish feasts. (Mark 15:6; Luke 22:1–2)

Additional guards were added to secure Jesus's tomb, which could not hold him. (Matt. 27:65–66)

5. Read Acts 12:6–11. How do we see God accomplishing Peter's rescue?

6. Read Acts 12:12–19, then look back at verse 5. What do you find a bit ironic in this passage? Can you relate in any way to those gathered in prayer?

7. Read Acts 12:20–23. When Cornelius tried to worship Peter in Acts 10:25–26, Peter refused his worship and said, "I too am a man," refusing to receive glory that belongs to God alone. How is Herod's response to being worshiped as a god in 12:20–23 different from that of Peter?

8. Read Acts 12:24. Why is this statement significant, considering the context of what we've read in chapter 12?

9. We're told explicitly that Herod "did not give God the glory." This sin is easy to recognize in someone who accepts others' worship—but perhaps it's harder to see this same tendency in ourselves. In a blog post called, "Photobombing Jesus—Confessions of a Glory Thief,"[1] Garrett Kell lists six ways we sometimes seek to take God's glory for ourselves.

- "I want Jesus to be glorified, but I want glory too."
- "Because I want affirmation, I hide my sins."
- "I become bitter when God uses others instead of me."
- "I become more concerned about my public performance than my private devotion."
- "I fear moral failure, mostly because it would defame Jesus, but also because it would defame me."
- "My desire to be something rivals my desire for Jesus to be everything."

Do you recognize some of these things in yourself? Circle the statements you can particularly relate to.

Spend some time in prayer, confessing the ways you fail to give God the glory. Ask Jesus to give you the grace to die

1 Garrett Kell, "Photobombing Jesus—Confessions of a Glory Thief," garrettkell.com, January 19, 2017, http://garrettkell.com/.

to the sin of seeking the glory that belongs to him. Praise him for leaving the glory of heaven and dying a humiliating death, taking upon himself our sin of stealing God's glory. Thank him for coming to save you from seeking your own glory. Cherish the truth that he now dwells in you by his Spirit, empowering you to forsake the sin of stealing his glory.

Lesson 10

All That God Had Done with Them

ACTS 13:1–14:28

1. Read Acts 13:1–4. Based on the limited information provided here, what ethnic and religious backgrounds do the five leaders of the Antioch church bring to the table? (See Acts 4:36 and 22:3–5 for additional details.)

_____

_____

_____

_____

According to verse 3 and verse 4, who sends Saul and Barnabas?

v. 3:

_____

v. 4:

2. Read Acts 13:4–12. This Jewish false prophet and magician calls himself "Bar-Jesus," which means "son of Joshua" or "son of salvation." What is his true identity as revealed by Paul through the Holy Spirit?

What two things lead to the salvation of the proconsul?

3. Read Acts 13:13–14. Compare this to 13:5 and 14:1. What do you notice about Paul and Barnabas's strategy as they go from city to city? Why do you think they do this? (Matt. 10:5–6; 15:24; and Rom. 1:16 may help.)

4. Read Acts 13:15–41. The sermon Paul gives in the synagogue in Antioch of Pisidia could be titled "Salvation in Jesus." Provide a summary sentence for each section of his sermon.

vv. 16–25:

vv. 26–37:

vv. 38–41:

5. Read Acts 13:42–47 and Isaiah 49:5–6. As Paul preaches the the message of salvation to "the whole city" (thereby including crowds of Gentiles), the Jews are filled with jealousy. How do Paul and Barnabas use this passage from Isaiah to respond to them?

6. Read Acts 13:48–52. How does this passage affirm the significance of both divine election and human response in regard to salvation? How does this reality seem to impact Paul and Barnabas?

7. Read Acts 14:1–7. Paul and Barnabas are met with murderous opposition in Iconium. What can we learn from their response?

8. Read Acts 14:8–18. How is Paul's "sermon" to the Gentiles in Lystra different from his sermon to the Jews and God-fearing Gentiles in Antioch of Pisidia (Acts 13:16–41)? How is it similar?

9. Read Acts 14:19–26. On the map below, trace the path Paul and Barnabas have taken so far in this first missionary journey (13:1–14:20) from Antioch to Seleucia, to Salamis, to Paphos, to Perga in Pamphylia, to Antioch in Pisidia, to Iconium, to Lystra, and to Derbe. Then trace the path they take back to Antioch.

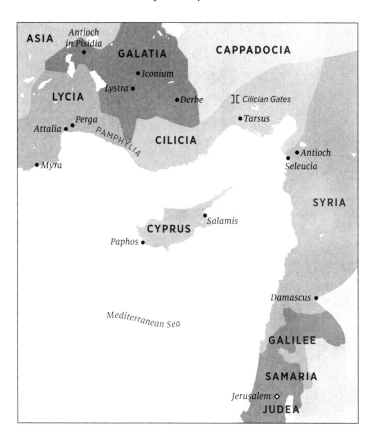

Why do you think they do not take the more direct land route from Derbe to Antioch of Syria?

10. Read Acts 14:24–27. In question 1, you were asked who sent Paul and Barnabas. Similarly, who did the work according to these final verses?

11. In this passage we see Paul and Barnabas experience murderous opposition. Yet we also see them return to places where they faced opposition in their mission to serve and strengthen the church. How does their example challenge or encourage you as you think about facing opposition or prioritizing service to the church?

Lesson 11

Saved through the Grace of the Lord Jesus

ACTS 15:1–16:5

1. Read Acts 15:1–2. How is this prerequisite for salvation different from what Peter and Paul have preached? (For help see 2:38; 3:19–20; 10:43; 13:38–39.)

2. Read Acts 15:3–5. What types of things would the Gentiles be required to do to "keep the law of Moses"? (Gal. 6:12 and Col. 2:16–17 may help.)

3. Read Acts 15:6–11. Summarize Peter's argument in each of the following verses:

v. 7:

v. 8:

v. 9:

v. 10:

v. 11:

4. Read Acts 15:12. How does Paul and Barnabas's testimony of the signs and wonders God performed through them support Peter's argument?

5. Read Acts 15:13–18, where James quotes Amos 9:11–12. What do you think it means that "the tent of David . . . has fallen"? (See 1 Kings 12:16–17.)

Toward what end will the Lord rebuild and restore "the tent of David"?

6. Read Acts 15:19–21. Why do you think the apostles and elders in Jerusalem determine that the new Gentile believers should abstain from the things listed in verse 20? (This is rather challenging to discern confidently from the text, so do your best. It will be clarified in the chapter or video session.)

7. Read Acts 15:22–35. Why do you think the Jewish and Gentile believers in the Antioch church would have rejoiced and been encouraged and strengthened by the contingent from the Jerusalem church?

8. Read Acts 15:36–41. Chapter 15 began with a disagreement regarding whether Gentiles should be circumcised that caused "no small dissension and debate." In these final verses, there is a "sharp disagreement" regarding ministry staffing. The earlier disagreement was a gospel issue. Do you think this disagreement has the same significance? Why or why not?

In what way is the outcome of both disagreements similar? (See v. 32 and v. 41.)

9. Read Acts 16:1–5. In chapter 15, Paul argued against circumcision as a requirement for Gentiles. Why do you think he now wants Timothy, a Gentile believer, to be circumcised? (Once again, this may be rather challenging to discern confidently from the text, but do your best. It will be clarified in the chapter or video session. Paul's approach to ministry as expressed in 1 Cor. 9:19–23 may be helpful.)

What does this passage reveal as the continuing fruit of the conflict in Jerusalem, Paul and Barnabas's conflict, and Paul's request of Timothy?

10. This passage has covered two disagreements and a significant decision that are all fraught with conflict. Conflict in the church can be incredibly painful, disillusioning, and disappointing. What do you think it looks like to work through

conflict in a way that strengthens the church and advances the gospel?

_____

_____

_____

_____

Lesson 12

There Is Another King, Jesus

ACTS 16:6–17:9

1. Read Acts 16:6–12. How do these verses demonstrate that Jesus is directing the spread of his gospel to the nations?

_____

_____

_____

_____

When Paul sees a vision of a Macedonian man saying, "Come . . . help us" (16:9), what does he conclude is the best way to "help"?

_____

_____

2. Read Acts 16:13–15. So far in Acts we've witnessed many supernatural events. What supernatural activity do you see in these verses?

What actions does Lydia take in response to the gospel?

3. Read Acts 16:16–18 and Luke 8:27–29. What similarities do you see? How does Matthew 12:22–29 help to explain what happens in Acts?

4. Read Acts 16:19–27. What are Paul and Silas doing in prison? What impact do you think this might have had on those around them?

_____

_____

_____

_____

5. Read Acts 16:28–34. How is the jailer's response to the word of the Lord similar to Lydia's response in verse 15?

_____

_____

_____

6. Read Acts 16:35–40. Why do you think Paul announces that he and Silas are Roman citizens and refuses to leave secretly?

_____

_____

_____

_____

7. Read Acts 17:1–9. In what ways are the charges against the believers true?

_____

_____

_____

_____

8. Work you way back through 16:6–17:9 and trace the action on the map below by drawing in the path taken by Paul, Silas, and Timothy (and Luke himself for some of it).

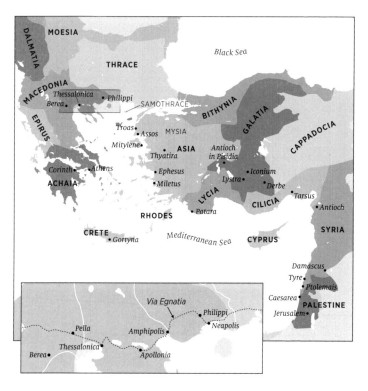

9. How has King Jesus turned your world upside down so that your life reflects his kingdom values? In what ways do your values or priorities need to shift so that they align with his kingdom?

_____

_____

_____

_____

I Have Many in This City
Who Are My People

ACTS 17:10–18:23

1. Read Acts 17:10–15. How does the response of the Bereans set a pattern and provide encouragement for all believers?

2. Read Acts 17:16–21. What is Paul's emotional response to what he encounters in Athens? How does he respond practically?

_____

_____

_____

_____

3. Read Acts 17:22–34. To what does Paul appeal in the Areopa-
gus? How is that different from the basis of his appeal in the
synagogue?

_____

_____

_____

What does Paul communicate about the purpose God is
working out in history in verses 26–27?

_____

_____

_____

What is the implication of the first coming and promised
return of Jesus for all people according to verses 30–31?

_____

_____

_____

_____

4. Read Acts 18:1–6 along with Luke 9:5. How do these two passages relate? What is being communicated by the actions described?

5. Read Acts 18:7–8. The Jews who rejected Paul's message could not have been very happy with the developments in these verses. What things are likely bothersome to them?

6. Read Acts 18:9–10 with John 10:16 and Ephesians 1:3–4. In what ways would the words of Jesus that Paul heard in his vision have emboldened him to take the gospel further into the pagan city of Corinth?

7. Read Acts 18:11–17. How is the Lord's promise to Paul in his vision fulfilled in these events?

8. Read Acts 18:18–23. Go back to the map in lesson 12 and draw arrows to complete the route of Paul's second missionary journey. (When we read in v. 22 that Paul "went up and greeted the church," he is most likely speaking of going "up" to Jerusalem, which was at a higher elevation than Caesarea.)

9. Everywhere Paul goes, rather than condemn, criticize, or ignore, Paul engages with people who see the world differently than he does and who have no hope in Christ. What do you think is your default mindset when it comes to interaction with the culture and systems around you where Christ is not honored? What could it look like for you to thoughtfully engage instead of condemn, criticize, or ignore?

Lesson 14

The Word Continued to Increase and Prevail Mightily

ACTS 18:24–20:38

1. Read Acts 18:24–28. Luke lists several very positive things about Apollos and his teaching. And he doesn't tell us specifically what Priscilla and Aquila point out to Apollos as being not quite accurate. What do you think Luke intends for his readers to take away from these verses about Apollos's ministry?

_____

_____

_____

_____

_____

_____

2. Read Acts 19:1–7. Paul explains to these men that Jesus is the person whom John the Baptist said would come after him. They have not heard of the Holy Spirit, which would mean they know nothing about what happened at Pentecost. What does this likely indicate about their spiritual condition?

3. Read Acts 19:8–10. Paul's missionary strategy has been to set up in a major city and send coworkers into the surrounding regions. How is that working now that Paul has finally been able to come to Asia, after being forbidden to do so years before (16:6)? How does that encourage you in regard to disappointments you've faced in serving Christ?

4. Read Acts 19:11–20 with Acts 6:7 and 12:24. How is the statement in 19:20 different from the others? In what way has the word of the Lord "prevailed" in 19:11–20?

_____

_____

_____

_____

5. Read Acts 19:21–27. Acts shows us how frequently false charges were brought against the apostles. But that is not the case here. What charges does Demetrius make against Paul that are true?

_____

_____

_____

_____

6. Read Acts 19:28–41. Earlier in this study we discussed the Pax Romana ("Roman peace"), which refers to Rome's approach to quelling riots and insurrection throughout the empire. How does the Pax Romana work in favor of Paul and the Ephesian church in this passage?

_____

_____

_____

_____

7. Read Acts 20:1–6. Trace Paul's route as he returns to Macedonia to encourage the churches he planted there and then sails to Troas.

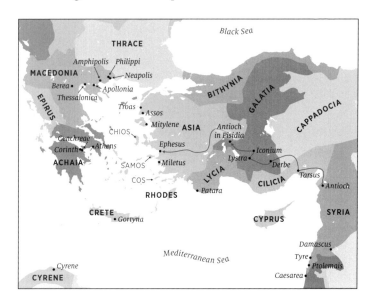

8. Read Acts 20:7–12. We might expect that the miracle of bringing a dead person back to life would be the most significant thing that happens on this Lord's Day in Troas. But based on what is repeated in the passage, what does Luke seem to want us to see as most significant?

9. Read Acts 20:13–16, continuing to trace Paul's journey on the map.

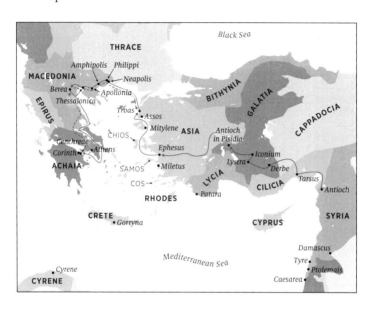

10. Read Acts 20:17–27 and 31–35. What are some characteristics of the ministry Paul has had among the people of Ephesus?

v. 19:

v. 20:

v. 21:

v. 25:

v. 27:

v. 31:

vv. 33–34:

11. Read Acts 20:28–38. What warnings does Paul give the elders? What does he commend them to?

Lesson 15

Paul Resolved in His Spirit
to Go to Jerusalem

ACTS 21:1–23:35

1. Read Acts 21:1–17, continuing to trace Paul's journey on the map.

What message does Paul receive from other believers as he makes this journey? What is his response, and how does that influence the believers?

v. 4:

v. 12:

v. 13:

v. 14:

2. Read Romans 15:25–31; 1 Corinthians 16:1–4; and 2 Corinthians 8:1–8. What do these passages reveal about why it is important to Paul to go to Jerusalem before going to Rome?

3. Read Acts 21:17–26. While Paul's ministry among the Gentiles causes the elders of the church in Jerusalem to glorify God, the thousands of Jewish Christians in Jerusalem have a problem with his ministry. What have they been told about Paul?

What remedy do the elders suggest?

4. Read Acts 21:27–36. Who stirs up the crowd and why?

5. Read Acts 21:37–22:21. Why do you think Paul tells those seeking to kill him for being "against the people and the law"

(21:28) about his own history of seeking to kill Christians and seeing the risen Jesus?

6. Read Acts 22:22–29. At what point are the people no longer willing to listen to Paul? How does this reveal the most significant issue they have with Paul?

7. Read Acts 22:30–23:10. What does Paul say is the reason he has been put on trial? Why does this statement create violent dissension amongst his accusers?

8. Read Acts 23:11. Paul has been put on trial before the council, and more trials and hardships are to come. Why would Paul

have been encouraged to hear that he "must testify" about the Lord Jesus in Rome?

_____

_____

_____

_____

9. Read Acts 23:12–22. How do these events demonstrate that the Jews are not really interested in the law of God being kept?

_____

_____

_____

10. Read Acts 23:23–35. What is the "verdict" of Lysias regarding the charges the Jews have made against Paul?

_____

_____

_____

11. While Paul is assured that he will testify to Christ in Rome, he has to wait a long time for that to become reality. Similarly, at the heart of what it means to be a Christian

is a willingness to wait for all of God's promises to become reality. What truths have you seen in Acts about God's character and how he works with his people that could help you to wait with faith for the fullness of what God has promised to his people?

I Always Take Pains to Have a Clear Conscience toward God and Man

ACTS 24:1–26:32

1. Read Acts 24:1–21. From these verses, what are the three "crimes" Paul is charged with? How does he respond to each of those charges?

Charge against Paul	Paul's response to the charge
v. 5a:	vv. 10–13:
v. 5b:	vv. 14–16:
v. 6:	vv. 17–19:

2. Read Acts 24:22–27. Paul reasons with Felix about righteousness, self-control, and the coming judgment. Why do you think each of these things might have caused Felix to respond with alarm? (A few notes that might be helpful: Paul would have written his letter to the Romans by this point, so you might consider his teaching on righteousness in Rom. 3:10–12, 21–26. Felix was known to be a cruel tyrant. According to Josephus, Felix seduced and lured Drusilla away from her first husband to make her his third wife.)

Righteousness:

_____

_____

_____

_____

Self-control:

_____

_____

_____

The coming judgment:

_____

_____

_____

3. Read Acts 25:1–12. While the charges made against Paul before Festus are not articulated here, we can make an assumption about the charges based on Paul's defense in

verse 8. What new accusation has been added to the charges made against him in the earlier trial before Felix?

_____

_____

_____

4. Read Acts 25:13–27. What does Festus make of the charges against Paul? What problem does this create for Festus?

_____

_____

_____

_____

5. Read Acts 26:1–11. What does Paul share with the Pharisees who are among his accusers? (See also Acts 23:6 and 24:15.)

_____

_____

_____

_____

6. Read Acts 26:12–15. What evidence for the resurrection of Jesus does Paul offer in these verses?

_____

_____

7. Read Acts 26:16–23. How does Paul articulate what it means to be saved in the following verses?

vv. 17–18:

v. 20:

8. Read Acts 26:24–32. How is Paul's interaction with Agrippa consistent with the whole of his ministry up to this point?

9. By the time Paul stands in these various courts, he has already written to the believers in Rome, "Let every person be subject to the governing authorities" (Rom. 13:1). How do you see Paul living out his own instructions? How does his example

challenge you as you evaluate your attitudes and actions toward governing authorities?

Lesson 17

It Will Be Exactly
as I Have Been Told

ACTS 27:1–28:31

1. Read Acts 27:1–28:1. Draw arrows on the map below to trace the journey of the ship carrying Paul; his companions, Aristarchus and Luke; his Roman Centurion guard, Julius; and another 272 people from Caesarea to Malta.

2. While Paul does not receive a miraculous deliverance from the stormy seas or ship that is breaking apart, he does receive supernatural revelation that gives him confidence. What is it?

How does he respond to this revelation?

How does this revelation relate to an earlier message from Jesus in Acts 23:11?

3. In Acts 27:20, Luke writes that "all hope of our being saved was at last abandoned." But Paul is "saved" from many things in chapter 27. What are they?

v. 24:

vv. 30–32:

vv. 33–36:

vv. 42–43:

vv. 44:

4. Read Acts 28:1–10. In what ways are these events also about the power of God to save?

_____

_____

_____

5. Though we're not told explicitly what happens on Malta, we could probably rightly assume a couple of things. Based on the events of Acts 14:8–15, how do you think Paul responds when the Maltese think he is a god?

_____

_____

_____

_____

Based on what Paul has done everywhere he has gone, and specifically during his two years in Ephesus (Acts 19:10–11), what could we assume is happening during Paul's three months on Malta in addition to physical healing?

_____

_____

_____

_____

6. Read Acts 28:11–23, continuing to trace Paul's route on the map found in question 1.

In what way is Paul's pattern of ministry in Rome the same as it has been everywhere else?

_____

_____

_____

_____

_____

7. Read Acts 28:24–28. Put into your own words what Paul communicates to the unbelieving Jews in Rome by quoting Isaiah 6:9–10 to them.

_____

_____

_____

_____

_____

8. While Luke is an excellent and careful historian, he is not simply writing to inform. He is writing to persuade. What do you think he wants his first reader, Theophilus, and his additional readers (including us) to believe and do based on the story he has told us in Acts? List at least four or five things.

_____

_____

_____

_____

_____

_____

_____

_____

_____

9. Throughout this study, we've seen the Holy Spirit at work in and through his people in many ways. How have you gained a greater appreciation for what it means to have the Spirit's power at work in and through your life? How could you cultivate more of an awareness or appreciation of the Spirit's work in your life?

_____

_____

_____

_____

Resources to Go Deeper
in Your Study of Acts

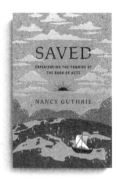

Saved: Experiencing the Promise of the Book of Acts

Saved Video Study (DVD or Download)

Saved Personal Bible Study (Paperback or Printable PDF)

Saved Leader's Guide (Paperback or Printable PDF)

ESV Scripture Journal: Acts (Saved Edition)

For more information, visit **crossway.org**.